Departures

Other poetry collections by Philip C. Kolin

Roses for Sharron (1994)

Deep Wonder: Poems (2000)

Wailing Walls (2006)

A Parable of Women: Poems (2010)

Reading God's Handwriting (2012)

In the Custody of Words (2013)

DEPARTURES
A Collection of Poems

Philip C. Kolin

MOBILE, ALABAMA

Departures

© 2014, Philip C. Kolin

Cover Design by Megan Cary
Interior Design by Danielle Sypher-Haley

ISBN 978-0-942544-25-1
Library of Congress Control Number: 2014950134

Negative Capability Press
64 Ridgelawn Drive East
Mobile, Alabama 36608
(251) 591-2922

www.negativecapabilitypress.org
facebook.com/negativecapabilitypress

for Ethlyn

Acknowledgments

I am grateful to the following journals and anthologies where some of these poems, or earlier versions of them, originally appeared:

After Dark: The Tavern Across the Street

Anglican Theological Review: October was Cracked

Avocet: A Eulogy for the Buffalo

Big Muddy: September Edges; Post Cards from New Orleans

Black Magnolias: A Delta Christmas

Blueline: God's Love

Cape Rock: Fermi in Black and White

Christianity and Literature: Teaching in Heaven

Copyright © 2013 by the *Christian Century.* "Adam's Three Gardens" by Philip C. Kolin is reprinted by permission from the July 10, 2013 issue of *Christian Century.*

Copyright © 2013 by the *Christian Century.* "Revelation" by Philip C. Kolin is reprinted by permission from the February 19, 2014 issue of *Christian Century.*

Crux Literary Journal: Tally Your Soul

Dead Mule: Farewell, Big Easy: A Katrina Dirge

Hurricane Blues: The Slaver Superdome

Indigo Rising: The Taxi Ride; Marriage; Leaves; Words

In the Custody of Words: pecata mundi; The Printers' Mass; Fish; The Prayer Lady; The Secretary

Louisiana Literature: Anniversaries

Negative Capability: Lucy

The Penwood Review: In the Waiting Room

Performance of a Lifetime: A Festschrift Honoring Dororthy Harrell Brown: Magistra Loyolensis

Pilgrim: A Journal of Catholic Experience: A Mother's Voice

The Prose-Poem Project: Sister Veritas; New Orleans, New Orleans

Poems & Plays: The Soddy-Daisy

Poetry South: A Winter Day on Panama City Beach

Saint Austin Review: Mother Teresa's Watch

Seminary Ridge Review: Paging Dr. Seuss

The South Carolina Review: Memorial Day on Panama City Beach; White Antelopes for Holly Stevens

Spillway: Kenny's Chill Pills

Subliminal Interiors: Perhaps; The Air Has Left Our House Dry

Third Wednesday: St. Michael the Archangel and the Puppies; Lunar Equations

Time of Singing: Emergency Lovers; At the Sack and Save

Valley Voices: Seduction Red

Praise for Departures

Whitman would love this book as much as I do. The big people walk through it—Katharine Hepburn, Sylvia Plath, Enrico Fermi, Mother Teresa—but so do the little ones. There's a cousin who was killed in World War II because he hadn't noticed that he'd wandered into enemy territory, for example, and a maiden lady piano teacher whom a young speaker spies when he gets up the nerve to stick his head in the neighborhood tavern and sees her perched on a barstool, "a wingless angel / pinned to her frayed cloth coat." *Departures* is as strong as coffee, as real as sin. It's the whole package and more. —David Kirby

Because "no one knows water / like a drowning man," Kolin, who understands, gives us a raft to cling to: a calendar of life, from youth, first love, the darkening of October, November loss, death, to the comforting knowledge of "God calling us back to paradise." Interspersed, the sins of our times—racism, Katrina, the Holocaust—but always the transformative power of love. Who could forget the widow who turns "an obituary / Into a love letter"? —Alice Friman

There was a time when all art aspired to praise, and there is much praise going on in Philip Kolin's poems, and much to praise about them. Which is not to say they are pious, because there's a lot of fun mixed in: nuns, the Sack and Save, fish, Wallace Stevens, the jazz of Bourbon Street, no matter the subject, Kolin is right at your elbow pointing out the revelations you see every day but don't notice. And these poems themselves will be revelations. Philip Kolin can think and sing at the same time. —William H Greenway

If such a thing as a Mohs scale existed for poetry, there's no doubt the poems in Philip Kolin's new collection, *Departures*, would rate high marks in all vital categories. There's unique clarity to his poems about childhood, brilliant luster to his poems about love, and unforgettable resonance in his poems on faith. Scratch the surface of any of these poems, clack them against the truth you know from your own life, hold them under the brightest of critical lights, and I'm sure you'll realize, as I did, they are the rarest of gems polished by the most gifted of jewelers.
—Jack B. Bedell, Editor, *Louisiana Literature*

Like Virgil in Dante's *Divine Comedy*, Philip Kolin's powerful poems introduce us to a wide variety of characters as they journey through their own heaven, purgatory, or hell. In exposing their individual dreams and fears, Kolin defines our journeys, too, in poems that act like mirrors in which we see ourselves. Whether it is the jilted woman who "decorates her walls with dust and frames the emptiness" or the prayerful voices honoring creation and the creator, Kolin's new collection reveals the wide ranging influences that shape his beautifully crafted new collection. I hear the Psalms, the cries for civil rights, the horrors of the Shoah, the penetrating paradoxes of Wallace Stevens, but also the joys of a recalled Chicago childhood, and the ebb and flow of the Gulf that Kolin loves so much. Readers will profit form the various types of departures from and into self in Philip Kolin's work. —Malaika Favorite, Writer and Artist

Philip Kolin's new book of poems, *Departures*, glides between the mundane and the magnificent, the evanescent and the concrete, with wonderfully sonic, perfectly calibrated yearning. In the dazzling poem, "Fermi in Black and White," the speaker testifies: "A law in physics states / a body can exist in time even when / the circumstances of its appearance / make it vanish." These poems possess a specter aura, a haunting valence rooted in an obsessive memory that reflexively conjures apparitions. They are, by turns, narrative, contemplative, showcasing the lyric precision of a poet whose ear is to the earth, eyes on the firmament, his hand over his heart as he prayerfully, often liturgically, recounts a past and present that exist simultaneously in the shape-shifting ellipses of recollection. —Joseph Bathanti, Poet Laureate of North Carolina

Departures reminds us from its outset that our *in utero* experiences are a departure from the "infinite." Engaging this central Augustinian paradox, Kolin tells meticulously crafted narratives that challenge us to reconsider the tensions in our own familial, romantic, and intrapersonal relations. This intuitive collection, among other achievements, is a much-needed validation of the power of story in our spiritual pursuits. —Martha Serpas

In *Departures,* Philip C. Kolin writes with elegance and grace about the leaps and shifts that mark a life, from falling in and out of love, to confronting racism, to surviving natural disasters, and finally to embracing the spiritual in the transition beyond the physical world. Here's an engaging and enlightening contemplative collection of poetry that will prompt you to examine your own significance in the vast and wide resonance of the cosmos. — Mary Swander, Poet Laureate of Iowa and author of *The Girls on the Roof*

Table of Contents

Childhood Encores

Casabas 1
A Delta Christmas 2
Paging Dr. Seuss 3
St. Michael the Archangel and the Puppies 5
The Taxi Ride 7
Sister Veritas 8
The Tavern Across the Street 9
For My Cousin Killed in Luxembourg, 1945 11
Fermi in Black and White 12
Why I Majored in English 14
White Antelopes for Holly Stevens 15
Memorial Day on Panama City Beach 16
Magistra Loyolensis 17
The Key 18

Women and Men in/out of Love

Moonvines 23
Odessa 24
Singled Out 29
Starched Ladies 30
Lucy 31
Ave, Kate 33
Sylvia Plath's Epitaph 34

Lunar Equations 35
Seduction Red 36
The 19th Century 37
Marriage 38
September Edges 39
Words 40
Brave October on the Beach 41
A Winter Day on Panama City Beach 42
Rivers 43
Kenny's Chill Pills 44
The Soddy-Daisy 45
God's Love 46
Emergency Lovers 47

Obsequies

Leaves 53
A Eulogy for the Buffalo 54
Drowning 55
The Prayer Lady 56
October was Cracked 57
Waiting for Beckett 59
In the Waiting Room 60
Perhaps 61
The Dead Speak 62
New Orleans, New Orleans 63
The Slaver Superdome 64
Farewell, Big Easy: A Katrina Dirge 66

Postcards from New Orleans 67
A Mother's Voice 69
Houses Also Cry 70
Anniversaries 71
The Air Has Left Our House Dry 72
Passover in the Camps 74

Revelation

Adam's Three Gardens 81
pecata mundi 82
The Performance of Waste 83
Revelation 84
Tally Your Soul 85
Fish 86
The Printers' Mass 87
At the Sack and Save 88
Sailing the High Seas with Wallace Stevens 90
A Date with God's Cousin 91
Mother Teresa's Watch 92
Teaching in Heaven 93
The Secretary 94

Author's Biography 97

ONE

Childhood Encores

Casabas

How much like a casaba
is Dorothy's ochred belly,
a soft winter melon growing
seeds inside rattling, waiting

for a harvest of more children
to fertilize the land that favors
their intimacies, arms reaching deep
into its tilled womb, loamed with fullness.

The pale green flavor of the casaba fills
seasons inscribed in white-columned ledgers
and in shacks shaded with plantain leaves
as sleep unshackles dreams of another

seacoast and farther mountain plains
where the golden sun arrives earlier, stronger
before it is softened
in the sweet sorrow of Dorothy's moans.

A Delta Christmas

Divinity in the Delta
Falling sugar, falling

Sugarcane hosts
Children catch them

On their tongues—
Runways for doves

Temple gifts for a birth
In the sweetgum night air.

Grandma Anna is praying late,
Stirring up Christmas

Hominy and incense—
A large smoking hog

Crackling earth's fat
Drifting pleasingly toward

The clapboard sanctuary
Quilted white

Welcoming chilly angels
To this world's weathers

Paging Dr. Seuss

The worse coughs come
After dark: every shadow speaks

With a torturous tickle, a small voice
Begging for water, light, breath.

Why can't Dr. Seuss cure a fever
Just by leaping off

The page? Even when tiny animals
Sneeze, he is right there

With his sugar-cured words
That soothe throats and lower

Temperatures. There is a bonfire
Tonight in his eyes and toes;

The bed sheets are ready
To burst into flames.

Call the fire department,
The newly appointed chief

Of the red wagon orders.
But 911 does not answer

The plastic phone. It rings
But does not talk.

Not all the ice cubes
In his Gatorade can cool

Him down. She rolls up
The window shade hoping

The street iced with sleet
Might make him feel better.

But all he sees is
Dr. Seuss leaving town.

St. Michael the Archangel and the Puppies

My aunt told stories to keep me
from being frightened at night.
Her neighbor Stephanie upstairs
regularly got beat up and her cries and pleas
trickled down the pipes
into my aunt's kitchen sink
like a slow leak.

These were the whining puppies
behind the stove, but I was not to look
for them. It was dark on the other side
and they needed to sleep.

But Stephanie upstairs did not sleep,
or not much anyway;
and besides maybe some day
I could give her one of the puppies
to cheer her up.

Every night my aunt would pray
to St. Michael the Archangel to chase away
the demons. I always feared they crawled
into her bedroom closet, hiding from
St. Michael whose wings stretched across Chicago.

As St. Michael battled against the devil's snares
I used to dream of the poor puppies and Stephanie
caught in his trap, sneering at them both,
and maybe at me fearing he would call the demons
out of the closet.

One night there was a fire in my aunt's closet and when the firefighters came to put it out all they found was Stephanie and the puppies turned into ashes.

The Taxi Ride

Venomous memory—my father
sitting in the back seat
of a taxi, me next to him.
I think it was a Yellow Cab.

Out of the back window branches
played billiards with the clouds.
I wondered if he bet on the outcome.
The sunshine was at stake for me.

The cab finally pulled in front of
my mother's fenced yard.

My father got out,
carrying a duffle bag
full of my unworn clothes;
my toothbrush was still
in its plastic coffin.

When he eyed my mother,
they put boxing gloves
on their words—
but there was no referee.

My visit to see him didn't last
as long as their fight
right there on the sidewalk.

Then my father got
into the Yellow Cab, waiting,
and drove away.

Sister Veritas

Sister Veritas read the Mayan calendar to her eighth grade class at St. Ludmila's School of Dance and Keynesian Economics. The louts among them smoked cottonwood cigarettes in the alley behind the Blue Island Avenue bus line. The fumes left hazy tattoos imprinted on their arms and chests but also promised red circle sunsets on Ember Days. Sister always made sure report cards, recorded in Mayan, of course, were embellished with brown fig leaves and ready for Fr. Quasimodal to hand out to the class when tidal waves reached their highest point in the lower Pacific, and the solar eclipse had transversed the Southern Hemisphere. The boys often sought comfort in wearing Hispanic names to her class. Though a martinet, Sister Veritas never insisted that they be removed.

The Tavern Across the Street

Never once did I dare to go
inside the tavern right across
from our apartment on 19th Street.

For seven years I read the sign
"Yousay Beer," blinking,
blinking through our blinds.

When the sewers backed up,
my mother blamed it on the tavern
for opening its doors too early

and closing so late.
The drunks' breath, she insisted,
polluted the neighborhood.

When I graduated from 8th grade,
and the moving van came to take us
away from the old neighborhood

where gang obituaries
made headlines every week,
I snuck inside the tavern

one afternoon just to see
how much evil lurked there.
All I found was Miss Regina

my piano teacher who visited
our apartment every Wednesday
evening at seven for my private

lesson and stuck a silver star
on my purple *Schwann* book.
She sat on a high barstool, a tall

Pilsner stein before her
and a wingless angel
pinned to her frayed cloth coat.

For My Cousin Killed in Luxembourg, 1945

To my cousin with the golden smiles
And wire spectacles that still hold
Your eyes for the next generation to see:

Why couldn't someone see that you couldn't.
Two feet away and you were
In another country? How much blindness
Did your draft board need to defer you
To marry at St. Lucy's?

We were both fed on the same stories and family
Dinners with dumplings as big as rain clouds,
Roasts with veins like bloody trenches,
Ducks with crisping skin and fat necks on Sunday,
And *kolaches* bleeding raspberry hearts.

You were kind, tall, wrote a good hand,
Won all the trophies of youth. Then Luxembourg—
A flame-thrower caught you in a tree.
You were like a Czech Huck Finn fishing for mushrooms
On warm Octobers in the Michigan forest preserves.

I could not attend your funeral; I was not born yet.
But I have your birth certificate, baptismal papers,
Your confirmation name, *Stephen,* all sealed in
cellophane. Your letters from Camp McCain
proved you bought war bonds.

All your medals have been left
to those who cannot wear them.

Fermi in Black and White

An old black man leaves
the white world his photo
when he was a teenager
taken by the *Chicago Sun-Times,* May 1944,
standing next to Enrico Fermi on the Midway Plaisance,
just by chance—

like an equation between
his south side reality
and the dark side of the moon.
The photo made him Fermi's black protégé,
part of Atomic History preserved

in a Glad bag enshrined in his pocket,
so the explosion of blood and words
would not erase him in the bars on 55th Street.

He bragged about how Fermi taught him
to speak white math better than all the brothers
at Hales Franciscan High School
bleaching the minds of colored boys.

In a flash he was white
admitted to museums and libraries
in D.C., San Francisco, Boston, Denver,
Alamogordo, Hyde Park, everywhere.

Robed in a photographic glow, his face
showcased on the cover of *Time.*
How much more white can you get than that?

A law in physics states
a body can exist in time even when
the circumstances of its appearance
make it vanish.

Why I Majored in English

I majored in English
to learn how to be polite
in front of cats

to swim in poems
meter after meter
deep

to tell stories about chimney-smoking
serial novels . . .

to disinvite magpies
to Capistrano and elsewhere

to save clouds in pajama
pockets for dreams, lots of dreams

to watch a girl at the library
comb centuries out of her hair

to be anonymous when I am near
seacoasts, rodeos, and church chimes

to translate rain into rainbows.

White Antelopes for Holly Stevens

White antelope bucks
clamored noiselessly
in the licorice night.

Her father took her
on a Ferris wheel ride
that made two or maybe
three sprinkled
stops.

She rode a white antelope
who ate motion
until her father's
laugh was disconnected.

He wanted to extemporize,
but the circus went
the other way.

Memorial Day on Panama City Beach

It's Memorial Day and every lamppost becomes
a patriot, flags flying in their lapels.
On Panama City Beach the girls
wear their new tattoos like medals
you don't take off. The ripples of the waves
wave to the lampposts that return the wave.
Even the sun recites the *Pledge of Allegiance* today.
Everyone could receive a medal, and the girls
keep texting. Maybe it's the waves
they're sending messages to—
to come home or go back, empty
without all that churning foam on shore.

But I'm moving away, like the waves, from the day
to honor the heroic, the brave, the free.
That's the message the flags send
to the waves that the girls text to—
whoever takes a message on a beach?
Maybe the girls' texting is an updated
version of finding a message in a bottle
that's been floating around the waves
for centuries. But the waves couldn't read
back then like the girls do now. And let's face it—
waves have gotten a lot smarter since 1776.

They're almost finished building the new
bridge across from Pier Park Mall, swanky.
They say it will have a row of flags on it
and girls with medals texting the waves
beneath.

Magistra Loyolensis

for Dorothy Brown

They gather in all their decades
The volumes of students
Whose texts of self and the other
You had gracefully edited,
Transforming script into Scripture.

Emma, Daisy, Blanche, Kate,
Edna, Adrienne, Sylvia, so many
Claimants for women's rites
Championed in your classes.

Your students learned the wisdom
Of an epicene warrior fed on spiritual exercises,
Leaven for the struggle against
A wordless void,
Flat and final.

In your classes they discovered
Life outside the parentheses of custom,
Freed from the psychology of hair,
And the chronology of expectation.

You taught the sweet ambiguity of absence,
And the danger of claiming presence
As the only refuge of thought.

You showed them archangels in the margins.

The Key

I used to carry a key
to the house where we vacationed
so many years ago,
coaxing the clouds to step
down so we could play
in their fluff and float, blowing them
away in their phantom shapes
high over the turtlenecked waves
of the Gulf of Mexico.

But the key is now at the bottom
of the landfill,
sharing its tombstone life with ghosts
from other houses, garbage
cans, cups, clothes without arms
or legs to give them a chance to escape,
a deluge of starving microwaves, plastic
bottles crushed.

No one comes home there anymore,
though the variegated sky never left
nor did the oleander bush,
blushing with its red boutonnieres.
Several neighbors' dogs continue to visit
the foundation and the driveway
streaked with cracks and interloper weeds.

The street lights come on, too, every night,
their poles still trying to catch
the clouds.

TWO

Women and Men in/out of Love

Moonvines

Like a covey of brides
They fly out—
A cotillion of white doves
Layered in Vermeer slips and petticoats,
Folds gathered inside folds inside folds.

Giddy virgins wearing silver earrings
Charming the night's shadows
Dance at an April feast surrounded by
Blue star sparklers on elm fingers.

They are out tonight with their pearl lamps lit, reaching
Toward the groom to pleasure his eyes,
Eagerness painted in their soft silk smiles.

But then the sun, jealous with yellowing age,
Melts the moon into memory
Sadly, slowly in his glaring daylight garden,
Drooping with jilted corsages.

Odessa

Thoughts of an 18 year old young woman of color living in New Orleans, circa 1939.

1

Black women cargoed for white pleasure,
chained for centuries to the ghosts
of grandsires refusing to recognize them,
mulattoed into the bondage of skin
their offspring still wince over
the thralldom of race.
How much more does it take to be white?
How much less does it mean to be black?

2

When she was twelve, Odessa learned
white boys can't give you white babies.
They will come out black no matter how
fair their faces or straight their hair.

Their birth certificates will be stained *"Negro."*
Once she kissed a white boy who reported her
to the sheriff; he threatened her
with indecent exposure of her feelings

3

Odessa could never fathom
why blacks seemed invisible
while whites strutted about like high noon.
White overseers had no trouble
aiming flesh-ripping barbs at blacks
who could never look them in the eye.

But Odessa lived in a twilight
world where neither the sun
nor night could make her disappear.

4

She dreamt that God whispered to her
as she lay in a valley of graves,
her bones withering away—

He promised to open her piney prison
and knit pearled sinews
all through her body. Then God loosed
the four winds of His breath until
she rose so radiant no eye could see her.

5

Odessa's Great-Auntie Rachel told her
not to forget she had more family
than those fancy surnames printed on invitations.
Told her to look inside before
she stepped outside so as not to be
blinded by that white glaze—
swamp gas hiding haints.

6

Lord, it took courage to pass for white
in Louisiana in the 1930s. The white half
extended only up to the back of the bus.
All the tired colored girls there
had to get off; only white ladies could primp
without changing their seats.

7
So Odessa moved to the white side
just to see how it felt; a drawling,
blond-faced rogue sat next
to her, a smile his calling card.

But when he found out she was feigning,
he hit her hard, then turned his back.
Now she's blue as well as black.

8
Her skin was the color of oyster milk
strained through honey; she brushed
her long auburn hair every day
and powdered those dark circles
beneath her pearl blue eyes, her tears
crystals on dimmed chandeliers.

9
A tinge of blue, a subtle shading,
an unfriendly light, a lingering glance
made her afraid to claim her double
heritage. When would the time come
she could avoid being imprisoned
in a legal record for merely being lovely?

10
"Too light, girl, you too light,"
her black friends jeered at her
for playing one of those chalk-faced
mistresses up on St. Charles Ave.
One back channel girl declared,
"Odessa weren't nothin' but a white outcast."
What colored boy wants a girl

who passed among the birches for white
and what white boy would want
a black girl who crossed
the color line?

11
Who defines race? Who measures
blackness? Who is the whitest?
Not all cane is pure sugar,
and not all rivers run dark.

Same thing Odessa said to herself,
living between two worlds,
daring to dance into the white one
with a half-fearful smile.

12
A new decade arrived and Odessa
with her velvet-soft voice
and onyx-beaded bodice
waits for a white man so much older

and lighter. She dances in his arms
and ponders a *developé*.
Should she commit to so much elegance?

The waltz timing saves both of them
the intimacy of revelation, a reverse turn
hurries them back into the line of dance.

13
The black Sisters of the Precious Blood
prayed to protect New Orleans from hurricanes,
floods, and fires, but were never asked to watch over
souls like Odessa who wondered why being part black

overshadowed her white ancestors.
Strange how their pictures hung in public places
along with her field kin whose photos
ended up on three-penny picture postcards

or in newspapers molting into heaps
of shadows. She dug up a few musty quarters
to send to the sisters, asking them to say novenas
to blanket her whole family.

Odessa's Envoi

*I wear a gingham dress made
from dyed cotton picked
and owned by my ancestors.
Solid to checks, checks to solids:
the heartbreak comes when they
force me to wear the one side only.*

*I bear many gifts
from Ethiopia and Europe:
teak, ivory, damask, opals.
In my veins flow the Nile
and the Congo, also the Seine,
the Tagus, and the Douro.*

*Ham and Japheth are my sons.
When my suitors look upon me
I am like henna and cinnamon,
crocus and lotus, I am
a lily streaked with muted jet.*

Singled Out

She was singled out and
did not know how
to turn intimacy into promise.

Once she dated a mason who drove her
all over town to see the foundations he laid,
pointing to them as if he were the father
of local history; she remembered
the cement side of their relationship
when it ended. How much romance
can there be in the Small Claims Court

Annex. Another time she fell
for a suave green card seeker
who promised her the planets
but figured she would settle
for a one-way bus ride out of Las Cruces.
She learned a new dialect of deception

when he left. She decorated her walls
with dust and framed the emptiness.
In every single room in her apartment
she shattered the mirrors.

Now only tearful frowns
and wrinkles stare back.

Starched Ladies

These women had long hair, braided,
twisted, tied tight at the back
of their heads, preventing men's eyes
from combing lusts through their thoughts.

In public staring places,
they hid among long-skirted juries
not giving an omer of attention
to worldly wonders lest a weighty decree
pull them into church whispers.

Inside their starched fortresses
their breasts were like silver
that no man could spend.
Honeysuckle words could not move them.

When disrobing, they stitched their eyes with hemp.
Mirrors were good only to caress Babylonian harlots—
eyes craving desire; desire craving eyes.

They pilgrimaged into lightning
flashes from heaven's camera
capturing them in ecstasy.

Tornadoes like steeple alarms
brought them hope that someday
the wind would carry them away.

Lucy

Lucy Mercer, Eleanor Roosevelt's social secretary, was FDR's secret mistress for years.

Lucy, did FDR ever drape
his black Yalta cloak over
you, hoping he could fulfill
the promise that his libido worked?

It must have been awkward
working for Eleanor by day,
wanting to love him by night.

Did you ever cross her name
off her stationery
to write your love notes to him.

I wonder if you and FDR
held each other's shadows
while she toured the world—
all those cold canteens and camps
painting her bucktooth stiff smile
on Pathé newsreels.

Did you guide his shaking hand
to make it write straight
on those letters to mothers
pleading to end the heartache
in the Pacific?

The day Europe surrendered
so did you.

All he bequeathed you
was a covert footnote in history.

Lucy, did he ever make you feel
like a woman who didn't need to come
under the cloak of a clearance
to visit his dreams?

Ave, Kate

Hail, Kate Hepburn,
Kate, with your bully blooming blush,
your Halloween hair
your apple Eve lips,
your cat-striped eyes,
your sweet sarcasm that could twist
anyone's smile.

Did Eleanor Roosevelt ever try
to impersonate you or
did you ever try to match her
with your photographic voice?

Your sharply sculptured face
belonged on Mt. Rushmore.
You were the Lady Liberty of Hollywood.

Kate, your beaux burned like bonfires
for your vanities. You went flying
with Howard Hughes.

You blew his advances away.

Kate, you were coveted by so many eyes
but Spence's could not be annulled to wed yours.

You hung on like winter dusk in North Dakota.

Sylvia Plath's Epitaph

He folded up
all his goodbye love
letters into a postcard
and sent it

to her, waiting
across a continent
of untried fears.

The day it came
she was reading the *Odyssey*.

On the subway
graffiti's billet doux
invited the touch of her eyes
in some erotic fantasy
underground.

She could no longer resist the mystery
of brazen wrists.

At home his words surrendered her
to poems that tasted like turpentine.

Lunar Equations

The soft midnight velvet sky folds
Into a cushion for the empress moon to linger
In dalliance this first night of the solstice

Winnowing away her more faltering duties
Of lighting the feeble and sallow-souled earth
Whose breath barely sustains a season.

On such a night she masquerades
As a gypsy dressed in dreams wearing a white cat
Purring in longing until the daylight shortens
To the limits of a cage

And pens in the fantasies
Farmers' daughters feed on
During winter's quivering light.

Seduction Red

The marketplace bursts into red
streamers of fleshy peppers

fiery as the sun in the middle
of fiesta during a late winter fast.

A woman with coins in her hair
dances as men with chipped smiles

watch and wager how many
of their desires she can fulfill

between their winks and cigar coughs—
her skirts tempt these deflated matadors.

Voices gamble for the señorita's favor;
the roulette ball jumps from white

to red. Later that night on the *Camino*
headboards are axed for firewood.

A soothsayer with patched eyes
predicts red-droplet rain.

He is licensed by the winds;
their message may come today,

or tomorrow.

The 19th Century

for Jimmy Stockstill

The 19th century was a fabrication of
    Arrogance and abnegation.
        Imperious hoop skirts wrapped
            Around pianoforte legs and
                Mustachio-tiered beards trapped
                    In florid, cautious skin,
                      Tepid winks.

The long century crept
    Like a disturbed lodger
        Awakened in the middle
            Of the body's muddle.

It caged poetry in:
    Draped the Crystal Palace in
        Brisk sonnets and
            Obsequies with opaque lattices
                Like a peacock's morbid desire.

Victoria Regina ruled over
    More Hottentots and Sudanese mullahs
        Than Yorkshire yeoman could compute.

Her empire multiplied
    Through semen and tears.

Marriage

A couple of paradoxes
Twinning yes to no.

Arrows and crosses
In the rings of life.

Seed and skin
Shape a pear.

Sun rays and
Moon pearls.

Fire searching for
Pools, pools

Searching for
Lapis lazuli.

Words large as boxcars
Small talk and fine print.

Wind and lighthouses
Beach umbrellas, anchored.

Lockets of hope, unfastened,
A wristwatch left

On the wrong side
Of someone else's dream.

Wrinkles are subtraction,
Wisdom's addition, too.

September Edges

We walk along the edges
Of this September Gulf
Wishing for more days of summer light.

Near the waterline an old man
Casts his fishing pole over
The shadowed sand hoping to catch
Just one silver fish.

We walk under his thin line
Between sundown and dusk
Asking how he's done.
"I've been feeding the fish all day,"
He chuckles.

Twenty minutes later,
We walk back; the Gulf air is damp.
A school of stingrays passes
In the moonless, dark water.

Like razors the old man's lines
Blow across the sand in the raw wind.

Words

Cloistered hands sew vows
Of sacred names into habits
Strong as armor, impenetrable
To throats hurling scoffs like rocks.

Lovers collect soft night flowers
As air does dew
To make each other's garden
A paradise won back.

The pianist courts time—
Her fingers whispering notes
Of intimate charms and grace,
Spells that colicky time can't mire.

In all these I find
The sweet strength and calm
Of you, of you.

Brave October on the Beach

As if betrothed to summer
Brave October struts
In hot-breath passion
Wooing the fickle wandering sun

Who has already adjusted
His course to bed with winter
On the approaching far side
Of the sky, just over

The horizon a squall of gulls,
With frost-coated wings flap, flap,

And cry like storm alerts.

A Winter Day on Panama City Beach

the yellow weather flag hoists
hosannas to the winter morning sun

a mustachioed widower tips his fedora
to the frilly waves reciprocating

with their taffeta smiles, rustling
glee at his courtship

Cistercian gulls process
in snowshoes imprinting prayers

all across the sands
blue plastic trash cans roll

over memories of summer's
empty bottles of suntan promises

a snowbird with a balding heart
hopes the winds today

will bring the fish closer
to shore where his net waits for

riches late in the afternoon—the sky
freezes into a rainbow of marbled saffron

at sunset the sea bundles
its waves for the long journey home.

Rivers

They flow like clothes lines
Across a country of shadows
Where lovers hang dreams,
Put up a prayer or two, or even a tear
Lengthening the suits of sorrow.

They look like folded hands
Crossing over encampments
Stirred with the longing of the world.

Music plays in them, too,
Still and sad, shriveled waves,
A procession of mourners.

But when a swaying wind
Conducts them in the moonlight
They turn into flowing symphonies
Dressed for an elegant night of revelries.

Kenny's Chill Pills

She left her first husband,
A staid and sorry-mongering calculator
Of mites and meanness,
For a Kenny Rogers look-alike—
An unmonied singer
Uncanonized in the pay of printed words
And camera shy unless two black Chows
Grew comfortable in his gray beard.
He could salt and pepper the winds
Into a soul-delighting roux:
He was honey-water swell.

And with this new man
She became a petal-soft flower
No longer a cold, perfunctory bedder
But a sugar-svelte lover, swept away
In betrothal dreams coming true.

She used to worry waves
Into her tight, budget-wound life
Until Kenny gave her chill pills:
The wind between his fingers
Clasping while opening hers.

The Soddy-Daisy

They starred in each other's fantasies
As permissive as bar smoke
In the shadows of the Soddy-Daisy
Where he stopped off
Before work let her go.

He'd buy her a slightly used rose
In peeling, plastic wrapping,
Less than two dollars for a dream.

The rose girl wooed customers
Between sales and bar stools.
As she passed him,
She wished his kisses were spoken
When he was sober.

When his Soddy-Daisy bride arrived,
They danced like the shadows
They thought angels make
On cinder block walls

Until he left her to go back home
To Florida, his ashes festoons for
Her coffined heart.

God's Love

Miss Dottie thinks God is a gentleman
As she arranges perfectly bound hymnals
In a row before the sanctuary.
He always rewards good manners, she insists,
And his order of service saves us
From the embarrassment of spontaneity.
He likes ladies to dress primly, church smart,
Even for Wednesday worship suppers.

At night, wrapped in a comforter
Woven by the ladies guild,
She talks to angels and sniffs
Bouquets of fragrant light
Sent by heaven's florist, the Holy Spirit.

Then she waits for God to woo her,
a gallant lover for a lady's spirit.
She longs to hear the flowers growing in his voice—
Blossoming canticles, sweet hyacinths.

Dancing through galaxies with him,
She imagines he enfolds her in a covenant of touch.
His heart beats the constellations into a Valentine,
Stopping time to turn her wishes
Into hand-holding prophecies.

Then he leaves, right before sunrise,
Just in time for her to perfume
The altar for Sunday morning services.

Emergency Lovers

She turned his obituary
into a love letter
recalling all the times
they embraced each other
as emergency lovers:

In the dead heat rushes
to the hospital for his strokes
and heart attacks; the broken dates
they had planned did not matter.
She still cocooned him in her arms
all those times she red-coded the nurses.

She entwined her fingers
in his wires, tubes, cries.
The pain-numbed love notes
his breathing sent sounded like sonnets,
or varsouvianas rhythmically
keeping time with his ventilator clicks.

Whenever he came home
they took mile-long walks around
the stories they shared about
their courtship near the end of the war.

The black voice of cancer nearly
silenced him. His arms had more
blue streams than Colorado
and more hooks and lines in them, too.

But he still spoke to her—
his words laced with absinthe,
morphine perfume.

A final disease turned him into an actor
taking many roles on his mind's stage:
a pantalooned game warden
thrashing the backyard for poachers,
a furnace-sighing gambler, prying loose
kitchen floor tiles like cards he wanted to deal
for the last round of their courtship.

When he played taps on Satchmo's trumpet,
she knew he had reached the promised land.

THREE

Obsequies

Leaves

November is the month of leaves.
Souls once bright in summer's folds
Fall into an embalmed crispness
Blown far away
From the trees that raised them.

They clutter my neighbor's roof
Annoy her sidewalk—
She sweeps them back to me.

I try to give them a kind burial.
Memories of shaded dawns and soft rain
Release family tears inside me.

With my brittle rake
I inter them in black plastic coffins
For the funeral procession
To the end of my driveway.
A thoughtful green hearse promises
To give them a fitting burial.

Is recycling reincarnation?

A Eulogy for the Buffalo

Their hides were stretched
Across the barn, salt dripping
From seams once holding pink flesh
Now hairy skeletons without bones,
A mortuary of desecrated animals.

Their spirits released somewhere—
Not here; their voices

Joined the litany of the wind
That scattered dust and their memory
Over the prairies, a giant bellows

Searching for a fire to enflame
Their pyre, the thunderous smoke a tribute
To their noble and fulsome stampede

Ended. The brute music of their hooves,
Kettle and bass drums, once pounded the earth
As if they were knocking on the massive doors

Of history demanding to go deep under—
Retrieving ancestors whose faces
Survived in caves and on the mouths
Of spears and shields, telling and
Retelling the ancient battle for survival.

Drowning

No one knows water
        like a drowning man

Its stubborn grip
        its fierce jealousy

Not to let any other element
        best it.

Always in competition
        for diurnal control,

The water tries to preserve
        what it owns

Bodies pickled in salt—
        shriveled apples in the foam

Until angry black birds
        smell tomorrow.

Famished by the sun
        they dare to pluck

The forbidden fruit
        of the sea

Thinking waves do not tattle,
        but they do.

That's when the sea,
        rolls its chest,

Pushing the man under. Only then
        does he know how a sunset feels.

The Prayer Lady

She was as thin as the wind
Skinnying through the slates
Of a picket fence around
An unweeded churchyard.

She couldn't wear petite anymore;
It layered up around her neck, her waist,
And bulged in places where she once lived.

They had to put her in little girls'
Smocks and hose as if
She were starring in silent films—

Replicas of what she would become
Except for the aura; that came later
With her visions of gray-cowled ancestors
Sewing for shadows.

A life of prayers sanded
Her lips bare.
She still interceded
For friends, family, strangers in pews

Who watched her shriveling away.

October was Cracked

1

October was cracked
early like a hazel
when white meat snow fell
announcing winter, soft, quick,
like silver bells ringing
through time.

2

would that she could put pain
in her pocket like love's
tarnished locket and all
would be well, but swelled
was her thought's docket.

3

it's the minds of the smart
ones, teachers, librarians, clerks,
who go fast, said the aide,
not knowing what
pain is left behind
in another country's pleasure.

4

Aunt Mollie's smiles
hide inside her wrinkles;
he remembers her
as his heavenly bride

5
deboned dust flies toward
the sun's shine scattered
and soiled in time;
then becomes an eternity
without rust.

Waiting for Beckett

The pale of the moon
Poured into his face

White with stark,
Cold, a self alone

Talking possibilities, but
Nothing could be done.

The carriers merit the bones and
Wear them like a mourning frock.

Boots lost look just like
Boots found.

A sexton's cord can be used
To pull out a breached child.

The train was late;
The station was so lonely.

Thousands waited for
The posting of yesterday's schedule.

It'll be on time.

In the Waiting Room

I sit in a waiting room.
Strangers hug the air
I breathe, a family
Of temporary space or

A flight of passengers stalled?
The air is recycled with coughs;
Sneezes like explosive words
Blow up sentences.

We suffer now as prisoners
In air that shackles our faces,
Immobilizing any trace
Of a smile inside our mouths.

But maybe we are still
In the terminal's morgue,
Shadows on a sheet of ice
Hoping for a sunrise.

Perhaps

Perhaps there was a reason for your call.
No requests will be refused.

The Paris cafés on the *Vieille Rue* are always crowded
In the crest of the moon.

We have pillow cases
From some of the most distinguished soothsayers.

Tears are predicted in your genome horoscope.
Keep your arms

Above your head unless
You need a pacemaker or a hanky
To cry away the sins of history.

Ohio is on life support.

For the sake of friendship
Watch your calendars.
Ensure all dates have a future.

Fear and trembling came upon me.
A watchtower unit suddenly became available.

Are you leaving?

The Dead Speak

The dead speak with nasal voices.
They do not worry about syllables.

Each spring the prioress orders
just enough bleach to whiten

all the flowers that stretch
across her Paschal garden.

Mulch and straw are removed
along with unkept vows.

St. Thomas Aquinas is read in dirty hallways,
and old basements.

In Tibet, ancestors gather at twilight
for bowls of tepid rice and incense.

If our souls were portable
would we hide them when we sin?

Walking home alone at night
the sexton wonders if he charged too much.

Ravens fade into relics
against a gray sky.

There are no exit signs
in heaven or hell.

New Orleans, New Orleans

They could not afford a trip to Europe. Instead, they settled on New Orleans. It had the graves, the monuments, the cuisine, the demi-denizens, the aroma of battlefields and bordellos, cobblestone poetry, the humidity of Africa, a river parting its curled waves down the center of the city, the prayers of the Ursulines forfending their congregation with hurricane lamps blazing at mid noon, sunsets more russet than the Baroness de Pontalba's cheeks when she entertained gentlemen in tricornered hats and bulging codpieces, cathedral bells that rang and rang but could not be tucked in, bridges that connected desire to death in the suburbs, streetcars transporting the embalmed ashes of Tennessee Williams at Mardi Gras, double equinoxes with a *prix fixe* menu, lusty redfish that were never served *sans-culottes,* pralines that melted into dark sugar air, wastrels escaped from Cleveland or Cairo who wrote poetry that never made it off a Pat O'Brien's cocktail napkin, black cats that roam balustrades, street dancers swaying to tambourines in their sleep, and who do not want to be awakened during a performance, Faulkner's bar tabs on display with no takers to pay them, bell jars of Katrina's left-over winds, Spanish grandees erasing French from street signs, French grandissimes erasing Spanish from street signs, antique shops that rent frayed, floralized furniture from the Cabildo, calliopes whistling like alarm clocks, the turnstile bar at the Monteleone where your destination is where you boarded, rum boogies that could annihilate the Moabites, carriages pulled by dryades and driven by the sons of the sons of the sons of the sons who harvested cotton, indigo, and cane, and who pointed out voodoo colors on shotguns on Rampart Street, and causeways that took them to the Levant, but only when the ground fog was thick enough to walk on.

The Slaver Superdome

Herded down like the black sheep
Of Internet America
They were sealed in the belly
Of the slaver Superdome for the rough passage
Through the privy of American dreams.

They were kept in chains
By government plutocracy;
White-collared stigmas
Booked their torture on the slaver.
Everyone looked like an addict
Hooked on despair in hip-deep filth.

Against the whipping winds
Spinning politician's lies
They heard the agonized cries of their ancestors
Who raised the levees, sowed rice,
Indigo, cotton, sorrow, and death
And had their bodies lifted up
As living sacrifices as they prayed for deliverance
On the fanless gallery of St. Louis Cathedral.

This time there was no deliverance—
The stench of history smothered compassion.
Federal hearts disconnected in their own chambers.
The white owners didn't even know
The slaver had sailed or how many
Shackled futures were slammed on board.
It was not a place to linger.

Hopeless down in the hole
They existed on rations of lies,

Slags of hysteria; they drank
The flotsam of anger.

Their nightmares exploded
In the captive air, swollen with coughs,
Throat-red rage, strips of flesh
Flailing like flapping tongues.

Descant helicopters discharged
Messages from phony abolitionists.
Black freedom was jettisoned
Once again over the side—
To accommodate marketplace suspicions.

A slave too old to survive
Died, slumped in irons. Millions of eyes
Bought the sight at auctions
Nationwide on white plasma TVs.

The slaver still sails across a sea of grief.
It is rigged again for the journey
In sister and brother ships
Docking in Houston, Detroit, Chicago.
Written on every manifest:
Destiny.

Farewell, Big Easy: A Katrina Dirge

The *Fugitivo* leaves at six,
Satchmo's last trumpet call.
Naked and empty, Marie Laveau's
Neighborhood of flesh, now sand.

Salt will inherit the wind—
Its taste will linger
On the tongues of time
Recording once there were

Twin pianos and all that jazz—
Children of the trombone,
Jeweled foreheads, and
Earrings that seduced sense.

In the storm all things change—
The winds erase cobblestone history.

Centuries are straw.

The jet plume mixes with the clouds.

Postcards from New Orleans

1

Everything in the city is connected
through sin or salvation:
from Storyville, amber Magdalenes watch
frocked spires from the bascillica
trying to convert the clouds over
the river to serve as acolytes
as the wrinkled curé reads
Holy Writ about the fervor of tongues;
the same clouds skirt back
down the Quarter's short
side streets to canopy
the temporary dwellers
in this lost paradise of the flesh.

2

Old Andy Jackson can still see,
but not ride to, the river—
filled with four hundred years
of history, bellowing tugboats,
and voices that voted for
and against him. He does not fret;
he has his Square filled with fickle pigeons
while the river counts its stone barges.
The one eyes and passes before
the other in an immutable procession.
The space between them a boardwalk
named after the Queen of Gazes.

3

The city tastes like coffee
deep, dark, redolent
chicory, a legacy and a reminder
that the dead are never far away;
they still sleep above ground but
often call upon each other through
the river and visit its underground
cafés, sipping black, mud-brewed brûlot,
skimming watery obituaries, waiting
for the next of kin and friends
to join them for their morning call.

A Mother's Voice

Your voice—close as sunlight,
a mother's care and comfort—
I wish I had saved it
in the family album.

Though far as the moon's morning
fading voices of the dead
softly recall small harvests,
the bounty of memory:

peddlers crooning about watermelons
on Saturday street corners;

staccato carrot slices laughing
in orange jello, a meager feast;

furrow-browed widows whispering
on narrow cemetery roads,
shouldering rented sprinkling cans
and small packs of fertilizer, replenishment

for the plots of earth where
their spouses grow in holiness.

In your voice today, I hear
the aching joys of paradise,
a mother still waiting

with sighing arms open
for her son.

Houses Also Cry

a reachless dwelling,
a house, a heart, hands

with no one to touch
unless you count door knobs

that open and close
every day the same

voices like paint
chipped and faded

they hide
in the walls, the halls

a table set for nothing
except stacks of want ads

no one has entered
two rooms of the house

in the last year, no one
has entered the house

unless by phone
and then only to cancel

a meeting, an appointment,
a get-together, no reason—

a wrong number

Anniversaries

A streak of blue in winter-sewn clouds
a faint outline of gray cowling the wind
a wisp of birds fine penciling the sky
dawn tapping with fragile yellow
on the first day after your funeral—
I calculate the calendars on which
your anniversaries will be inscribed,
each daily square becomes a flowerless grave
awaiting planting a memory.

The Air Has Left Our House Dry

The air has left our house dry
As her eyes three days after
He died.

The windows she nailed
Shut to the shaded sill.
No one can open them,
Not even the light

Comes home anymore.
She told it to play outside—
There's just too much reflection
Going on inside.

She put gauze in her nostrils
So the smell of his voice,
Perfume, robe, smoke, etc.
Can't reach her—
Memory is an ashtray.

She called the weather station
To request a hurricane,
Or something larger, to visit soon.
There's plenty of time now
For sisters and daughters
To bring havoc.

Her grandchildren ask her
To define him, i.e.,
Into how many parts
Could he be divided—
They want their inheritance.

She gave them his cigar bands
Saved over the years
Like a baby's locks.

When night arose
She heard the stars
Clink and clank like his old Studebaker
On their first date.

She decided to wear
Sunglasses after sunset.

Passover in the Camps

The twelve tribes of Israel gather at
Auschwitz, Bergen-Belsen, Buchenwald,
Dachau, Mauthausen, Plaszów, Ravensbrück,
Sachsenhausen, Sobibor, Stutthof,
Treblinka, Theresienstadt.

The inheritance of the righteous.

The Seder feast of blood, broken
bones, bits of lung coughed up, gouged
eyeballs, whelps of flesh howling,
fingerless hands, peeled skin,
hair plucked like corn on the Sabbath,
skulls filled with holes, bitter herbs.

Twilight is slaughtered like a lamb.

The garden—the Appelplatz—
sewn with bodies, standing room only,
woes gagged, roses growing across
the Kommandant's villa. Beauty strives
to breathe even in Shoah.

Great art Thou, Creator of the Universe.

Kapo Judas plants a kiss of twisted crosses
on the Messiah's lips. *The pay is good.*
They're not as bad as everyone says.
They're worse than everyone says.
But it's a lot of money.
30 Reichsmarks and all the horrors your eyes
can stomach. Food scraped from garbage can lids.

Your descendants will be more numerous than the stars.

Informants and the SS sit by cold fires.
A fugue of death makes the camp howl.
"Es ist Bach?" "Nein. Mozart."

Everywhere ashes like greasy snow douse
the camp as well as those outside.
A candy rooster from a neighboring farm crows—
starving Maccabees grab the wires
for a taste of his wings. We have learned
the folly of *Arbeit macht frei.*

The only freedom the SS delivers is in smoke.

Caiaphas, who conceals his star
under his Swastika-black conscience,
slinks off to the Oberführer
with his hosed confessions. Late winter
and the bodies, buried last spring, must be
dug up and burned, a campfire party in hell.
If they cannot work, let them rot.

*Still, the tombs will open and the dead
will rise and enter the city.*

Sonderkommandos mine for gold in the hills
above Jerusalem. Heinrich Müeller,
Hitler's satrap-in-chief, hides
in a Jewish mass grave,
the Berlin-Mitte Cemetery desecrated.

*I know the blasphemy of them which say
they are Jews and are not.
They are of the synagogue of Satan.*

So many strange blossoms
this time of year: yews, box,

willows, olives. Who knew
palms grew in Poland in March?

Deep within the SS's "Little Castle"
the Messiah's mother sends an angel
to find anyone who still has a tongue,
or an attached head, to wail
her son's misery. The worst tortures
always end in silence.

Who will sing Kaddish for those entombed in the winds?

Just after dawn, a rifle screams down
an old woman who meant nothing
to the Kommandant. Each day
the targets come closer.
The chazzan whispers: *"May God give
a lifetime to the family of Israel."*

Pilate washes his hands at Wannsee.

FOUR

Revelation

Adam's Three Gardens

The first resplendent and holy, flourishing
over waters, trees with fulsome fruit,
witherless leaves,
psaltery furrowing
the land, a covenant of light and mist;
no want; creation swelling, begetting
in the shadow of white-clifted wings.

In the second, sin sprouted
rocks and spurs; acorns detonate
like grenades; mandrakes scream
bloodroots and tribulation;
serpents untangle from
dead boughs,
sunlight shriveled up everywhere.

The third the garden within
tending memories of rock roses, fallen
pomegranates and sallow sunsets;
olive trees weeping in the wilderness
blood-seared thorns and stargazer lilies
pressed into a crown; God calling us
back to paradise.

PECATA MUNDI

bitter apples and serpent tricks, fig leaves,
loincloths, recriminations, wounded tongues,
banishment into the kingdom of shame
excursions through unfallowed time
firstlings with slit throats, anger's mark—
wizened olive trees, shrouded stars, roaming
wolves, frogs, goats with three eyes, unhallowed
bulls, carvings, gold, stones demanding worship
the power of scarecrows in cucumber beds
proud horsemen, signet rings cracked,
unoiled heads, molting horns against
the uncircumcised land keening
bare threshing room floors
pilaged seeds, festering sprouts
water bitter as wormwood
the inheritance of light, darkened
in Rahab's rambling, rusty smiles
sheets laced with husks, sullied with swill,
men with thin souls hoard dust and shadows
sell their bones for firewood and their eyes
for rich men's buttons.

The Performance of Waste

Has the sky shrunk?

Cities are corrupted by brine and dust,
fleas, mites, moths, ticks, splinters, toad teeth,
blind fruit flies, wingless sparrows,
flecks of sheetrock flung
from dying houses,
acid rain eating wormholes on tombstones
pelting windshields and neoned gabled roofs,
leaving greasy smears.

Waste has become a study for exhaustion.
Paper has been declared officially dead.

A sign at the Museum of Sexuality warns:
Don't mount the exhibits.

Revelation

At the end of time
everything trembles and topples—
the sun dresses in sackcloth,
plagues run amok, vaccines sour;
threadbare bones like oakum unravel
and children frieze into sandstone;
patriots fall like falling stars,
and the tower of the winds decays in stillness;
a flood of faces bloats the river
and suicides surface like bubbling sores.
Then holy men and women scatter
sainted salts to ward off
fiends trying to steal family voices
pleading for sanctuary; none left
but a remnant of martyrs
to scribble with blood and sickles
in bitter books about the end of time
until the kingdom of eternity reigns
salving the wounds of memory.

Tally Your Soul

Infants know more about the infinite
having just arrived from there.

Science aims at disproving
the paradoxes on which love rests.

Poets and prophets love the fog;
they can see through wet curtains.

The best way to strengthen your soul
is to stretch your voice in a thicket of butterflies.

Laughter in holy places
should sound like gazelles grazing.

If you take a tally of your soul,
don't do it like the Census Bureau.

Fish

for Sandra Leal

Born in water
with their eyes open
their sleek skin speckled with roses
their mouths breathing
the mystery of air
in cobalt rooms
Ichthus gloriosus
the motto of Christ
hosannas across
oceans and rivers
feeding the inexhaustible
multitudes while the shepherds
of the sea throw out
their crosiers to reel in
souls sealed for eternity.

The Printers' Mass

2:30 am, 32nd St., Manhattan, 1934

The Mass for souls who cross
liminal boundaries of night
and dawn, work and revelry, ink and
space.

Typesetters printing tomorrow's
stories of loss and love, sky and sorrow,
their hands immersed in mutabilities,
escape an off-key time clock
that clicks as much forward
as back.

Cabbies, wiping fatigue off their meters, stop seeking
fares and faces in this city of clouds and fumes,
leave their headlights on, double park,
double park on a narrow street of horns

Still playing for inebriated and transient
parishioners in tuxedos and toupees, swishing
taffeta skirts perfumed with rum and cola,
who slope toward an encounter with eternity
in this yawning hour.

Finally come the actors
seconded from Broadway stages
their roles still visible, costumed for
another century, another epiphany.

At the Sack and Save

I rush down the aisles
Gulping the anxiety
That feeds my hunger to get finished—
I make it to the checkout lane.

The old man ahead of me is
My cross; he is too slow.
He pauses with each item he saves
On the conveyor belt to be delivered
Into the billowy, white plastic wombs
Waiting for his massive hands.

He looks like what he buys—wrinkled,
Pocked cans at reduced prices, bread too old
To sell for today's hurried mouths.
Tassels grow out of his scalp
Like frayed skirt covers on the couch, sagging
At the Salvation Army mission.

It takes him an eternity to get it all.
I cannot wait anymore;
I am on a rigid schedule.

I snarl politely at the cashier
As I march like Holofernes out the door
To the parking lot, my cart a battering ram
Against the wind and the wait.

As I load my trunk,
There he is, pushing his cart
And smiling at me as if I were his son.

His voice kisses me as he wraps me in his words,
"God bless you and your family."

I think I'll see him again
When time is discounted.

Sailing the High Seas with Wallace Stevens

There it was—white and masted
like a Phoenician bark
moored on Westerly Terrace
until reveries stirred a breeze
that morphed into a gust.
Gunwales and hatches open,
Mr. Stevens sets out to tame the narrows.

Puffed up in pleats and stripes,
he charts the grass, waving outlandishly.
Summertime has become too riotous
to keep outdoors. Better off quartered
in the unexplored regions of the eye
where his voyage seems more seaworthy.

On the high seas
a gray green sky tumbled rills
far beyond the rapture of a rose garden.

A Date with God's Cousin

Sister Bertha will be 97
and knows the history of shadows
and the way the light is
aslant this time of year.

Her heart has already left
for heaven, but her mind wobbles
here as the fading *Angelus* bells
call the congregation, calling
them to today's soul's rest.

She prepares for a date
with God's cousin; he's the smart one
with light blue hair and cumulus whiskers—
his cheeks swell with persimmons.

In a few hours he'll sit with her
under the convent's shady ginko tree
and let her peek inside
his dance card.

She wants to try a new step with him,
the one she learned in Foxtrot vows ago—

the Fall-Away.

Mother Teresa's Watch

The Tigris and Euphrates
Smile softly across

Her face, like a sunrise
Before Eden

Fell and soiled
The sky.

She carries a crucifix
On a sundial that never darkens.

Her prayers reach
Beyond the time

Of diminishment—
All those cries

From lepers lying
On straw pallets

Like nails piercing
Their tattered flesh.

She wraps her arms
Around them,

A *Pietà* of comfort
In a city of sores.

Teaching in Heaven

for H. B.

Professor Howard passed in his sleep
Into a new university where he now teaches
Eternal English to angelic auditors
Whose prose style is Miltonic crystalline
And who don't trouble him about office hours,
Withdrawal slips, those infernal missed
Quizzes, exams, final grades, or incompletes.
Yes, while Professor Howard's earthly dolts
Whine like swine at homecoming time,
His new students bring him florilegia
Composed in sunshine sentences and
Cloud-capped letters.

The Secretary

for Loretta

She knew only as much theology
as could be pasted inside
the purple blue covers of
the *Baltimore Catechism*,
1941 edition. Yet her life read
like the *Summa Theologica*,
a meek Chicago secretary who heard God,
spent time with the angels at holy hours,
and talked to saints on bus rides
back and forth to work every day
for 33 years. She was martyred
by pinstriped despots who stood over her
typing their orders, returning their rancor
with smiles and *Hail Mary's*, spreading
the Kingdom at the Merchandise Mart
where she knew why God made her,
and where she willed good to everyone.
From her seventh floor office she could almost see
the Beatific Vision.

Author's Biography

Philip C. Kolin is the University Distinguished Professor in the College of Arts and Letters at the University of Southern Mississippi where he is also the editor of *The Southern Quarterly*. He has published more than 40 books on Shakespeare, Tennessee Williams, Edward Albee, Adrienne Kennedy, Suzan-Lori Parks, and other playwrights plus several collections of poetry. More than 200 of his poems have been published in journals and magazines such as *America, African American Review, Spoon River Poetry Review, Saint Katherine Review, Michigan Quarterly Review, Spiritus, Christian Century, South Carolina Review*, etc. He has also published a widely-used business writing textbook, *Successful Writing at Work,* now in its 10th edition with Cengage/Wadsworth. Kolin is also the publisher/editor of *Vineyards: A Journal of Christian Poetry* (www.vineyardspoetry.net).

www.ingramcontent.com/pod-product-compliance
Lightning Source LLC
Chambersburg PA
CBHW021014090426
42738CB00007B/785